To

From

A
KISS

COMPILED BY ROSEMARIE JARSKI

SIMON & SCHUSTER
New York London Toronto Sydney Tokyo Singapore

TO MUM AND DAD WITH THANKS AND KISSES

SIMON & SCHUSTER
Rockefeller Center
1230 Avenue of the Americas
New York, New York 10020

SIMON & SCHUSTER and colophon are registered trademarks
of Simon & Schuster Inc.

Designed by David Fordham
Picture research by Jennie Karrach
Typesetting by SX Composing Ltd, Rayleigh, Essex
Printed in Belgium by Proost

10 9 8 7 6 5 4 3 2 1

Library of Congress Cataloging-in-Publication Data

Jarski, Rosemarie.
  A kiss / Rosemarie Jarski.
      p.   cm.
  ISBN 0-671-88687-8
  1. Kissing—Literary collections.   I. Title.
PN6071.L45J37   1994   93-37799
394—dc20   CIP

Previous page: AN ALLEGORY WITH VENUS AND CUPID
(DETAIL) *by* Bronzino, *c.* 1540

PSYCHE REVIVED BY THE KISS OF LOVE *by Antonio Canova*, 1793

Egyptian relief

PREFACE

BIRDS do it. Bugs do it. But only you and I do it for love. Kissing has evolved through primitive tribal rituals, by way of troubadours, courtly love and Hollywood, surviving en route religious bans, anti-kissing leagues and garlic-dip to become what it is today: the most perfect expression of love between two human beings.

A kiss expresses other emotions, of course. There are kisses of friendship, respect, treachery, victory, peace, luck – every lip service from the Kiss of Life to the Kiss of Death. But the kiss of kisses is surely the one 'when soul meets soul on lovers' lips', the Kiss of Love. That's the kiss we all dream of, the kiss we're all out there trying to catch: life is one long game of kiss-chase.

Netted and pressed like so many butterflies between the leaves of this book are kisses galore. Open any page and out flutters a beauty, kissed back into life by the warmth of your sweet breath. I can't promise it will be your dream-kiss but be sure it has, like its kissing cousins, been hand-picked and road-tested for its powers to quicken your pulse and send tingles down to your toes.

Some of these toe-tinglers will reawaken memories of kisses-past – first love, perhaps, or an old lover long-forgotten; others, less familiar, will spark ideas for kisses-future. (Xxxperiment!) The best kisses, as always, will be those that take you by surprise.

The kisses in this celebration cross creeds, colors, centuries and continents, the real world and the reel world. Not all are masterpieces. Which doesn't mean they have nothing to say. A bubblegum-pop lyric about kissing may strike a chord in our hearts as resonantly as may a revered Shakespearean sonnet. In music, in literature, in art – in life, kisses are democratic. There should be no pecking-order where kisses are concerned. Kiss your mom. Buss your boss. Canoodle with your poodle. All kisses are worthwhile. Smmmooch your lover. But some kisses

KISS II by Roy Lichtenstein, 1962

are more worthwhile than others.

So, apart from sore lips, what's the sum of all these close en-counters? Kiss + Kiss = Bliss.

No matter if you've found your dream-kiss or you're still hot on its trail, this treasure-store of kisses offers blissful inspira-tion for all. I kiss you and leave you to its mouth-watering trea-sures. Happy kiss-chasing!

A Chivalresque Scene *by Ettore Tito, c. 1925*

KISCELLANY

1 A kiss is only ever a pucker away.
2 A kiss is never innocent.
3 A lisp is no impediment to kithing.
4 A kiss with a beard or moustache is generally a matter of personal preference. By and large, though, most men tend to prefer their girlfriends cleanshaven.
5 No need to keep a kiss in the 'fridge. It never goes stale or limp, never passes its kiss-by-date. Each one comes freshly-minted, hot off the press.
6 You can't kiss and whistle at the same time.
7 You can run out of sugar, you can run out of milk, but there is no recorded instance of a person ever running out of

kisses. Be suspicious, therefore, of the neighbor who knocks on your door at midnight claiming to be fresh out and begging to borrow some of yours. (Unless, of course, they happen to be lip-lusciously kissable, in which case invite them in, take your chewing-gum out, put your lips together, honey, and POUT!)

8 Frustrated kissers: if you're small but like 'em tall – get a pogo-stick.

9 If it ever comes to a choice of weapons, choose a kiss.

10 Kiss goodbye even when you're not going anywhere.

ROSEMARIE JARSKI

Y ou want to know how many kisses would be enough
    for me, Lesbia?
The number of sand grains between the tombs of Libya's
    ancient lords and the temples where Egypt worships
    Jove in the shape of a ram.
The number of stars that watch the furtive
    love affairs of humankind
    while the night is passing over them in silence.
That's how many would satisfy your crazed Catullus.
What can't be counted can't be an unlucky number.

Catullus, c. 84-54 BC *Poem VII* tr. *Jacob Rabinowitz*

ROMAN MOSAIC

Hollywood's the place where they'll pay you a thousand dollars for a kiss and fifty cents for your soul.

Marilyn Monroe

MARILYN MONROE AND TONY CURTIS *in Some Like it Hot, 1959*

PURPLE HAZE

P URPLE haze are in my brain,
   Lately things don't seem the same,
Actin' funny, but I don't know why,
'scuse me while I kiss the sky.

Jimi Hendrix, 1942-70 *Purple Haze*, 1967

JIMI HENDRIX *by Elliott Landy*, 1968

LOVER'S GIFT

I LED him to the grassy bank, wiped his body with the end of my silken mantle, and, kneeling on the ground, I dried his feet with my trailing hair. When I raised my face and looked into his eyes, I thought I felt the world's first kiss to the first woman, – Blessed am I, blessed is God, who made me a woman. I heard him say to me, 'What God unknown are you? Your touch is the touch of the Immortal, your eyes have the mystery of the midnight.'

From a short story by Rabindranath Tagore, 1861-1941

LOVE NIGHT, A LAOTIAN GALLANTRY *by* J. *Buckland Wright*

Haiku #102

Your kiss sensual
as wet moonlight licking an
ocean's naked waves

Kalamu Ya Salaam, contemporary

THE KISS OF THE WAVES, *Berlin plaque* c. 1890

. . . YOUR kisses are a drug, your mouth the urn
dispensing fear to heroes, fervor to boys.

Charles Baudelaire, 1821-67
from Hymn to Beauty, Les Fleurs du Mal., 1857 tr. Richard Howard

GRETA GARBO AND JOHN GILBERT in Flesh and the Devil, 1926

O H, innocent victims of Cupid,
Remember this terse little verse;
To let a fool kiss you is stupid,
To let a kiss fool you is worse.

E. Y. Harburg, 1898-1981

CUPIDS *by* E. M. Munier, 1894

So I kissed Lucy, and was very surprised to feel her tongue pop out. It was my first real snog and I loved it. You can imagine that I fell in love instantly. Sadly the next year Lucy developed distemper and had to be put down.

Stephen Fry & Hugh Laurie, from the book A Bit More Fry and Laurie, 1991

Elliott Erwitt, 1968

On Kissing

Wʜᴇɴ the lips of two lovers are brought into direct contact with each other, it is called a 'straight kiss'.

When the heads of two lovers are bent towards each other, and when so bent, kissing takes place, it is called a 'bent kiss'.

When one of them turns up the face of the other by holding the head and chin, and then kissing, it is called a 'turned kiss'.

Lastly when the lower lip is pressed with much force, it is called a 'pressed kiss'.

There is also a fifth kind of kiss called the 'greatly pressed kiss', which is effected by taking hold of the lower lip between two fingers, and then, after touching it with the tongue, pressing it with great force with the lip.

The Kama Sutra of Vatsyayana, 3rd century AD
tr. Sir Richard Burton and F. F. Arbuthnot

Tᴀɴᴛʀɪᴄ ᴀʟʙᴜᴍ ᴘᴀɪɴᴛɪɴɢ, *late 18th century*

Josef Kondelka, 1973

G REET one another with a holy kiss.

The Bible, Romans 16.16

A KISS IN THE RAIN

ONE stormy morn I chanced to meet
  A lassie in the town;
Her locks were like the ripened wheat,
  Her laughing eyes were brown.
I watched her as she tripped along
  Till madness filled my brain,
And then – and then – I know 'twas wrong –
  I kissed her in the rain!

Oh, let the clouds grow dark above,
  My heart is light below;
'Tis always summer when we love,
  However winds may blow;
And I'm as proud as any prince,
  All honors I disdain:
She says I am her *rain beau* since
  I kissed her in the rain.

Samuel Minturn Peck, 1854-1938

34

Y

YOU-ME *by* Ay-O, 1976

KISSIMILES

I T [kissing someone] was like putting your mouth against an automatic bank teller, where it swallows your credit card.

John Updike

W HEN she kissed him, he melted like a lump of milk chocolate.

Marge Piercy

K ISSING her lips was like kissing warm but uncooked liver.

Stephen King

KISSIMILES

It [kissing] was like diving off a spring-board.
Daphne Du Maurier

His kiss was like white lightning,
a flash that spread, and
spread again, and stayed.
Henry James

Kissing him would be like kissing barbed wire.
Rosemarie Jarski

ALL MY LOVING

CLOSE your eyes and I'll kiss you,
Tomorrow I'll miss you,
Remember I'll always be true,
And then while I'm away,
I'll write home every day,
And I'll send all my loving to you.
I'll pretend I am kissing,
The lips I am missing,
And hope that my dreams will come true,
And then while I'm away,
I'll write home every day,
And I'll send all my loving to you.
All my loving, I will send to you,
All my loving, darling, I'll be true.

Lennon and McCartney, 1963

LOVE LETTERS (DETAIL) *by Stanley Spencer, 1950*

H E pulled her closer and kissed her, gently, carefully.
'Your lips taste of apples.'
'Oh Henry, I love you so much, I'm so happy–'
'This grass is bloody wet,' said Henry. 'I suppose
it's the dew. Is it the dew?'

Iris Murdoch, b.1919 *Henry and Cato*, 1976

TWO NICE PEOPLE FALL IN LOVE, *by Kurt Hutton, Picture Post* 1953

KISSES MAKE MEN LOATH TO GO

MY love bound me with a kiss
    That I should no longer stay;
When I felt so sweet a bliss
    I had less power to part away:
Alas, that women do not know
Kisses make men loath to go.

Yes, she knows it but too well,
    For I heard when Venus's dove
In her ear did softly tell
    That kisses were the seals of love:
O muse not then though it be so,
Kisses make men loath to go.

from Robert Jones's *Second Book of Songs and Airs*, 1601

THE PALE COMPLEXION OF TRUE LOVE (DETAIL)
by Eleanor Fortescue-Brickdale, c. 1890

NECKING

Eve Arnold, 1965

PECKING

Richard Kalvar, 1976

All the Fun of the Fair

ROLL on up see the main attraction!
Head over heels all the fun of the fair!
Catch a ghost train to the haunted castle!
Ride a helter-skelter! Jack is waiting there.

Jack-the-Lad is waiting there,
The fairground king with greasy hair.
Ride at your risk! He'll steal your kiss!
Jack-the-Lad the fairground man.

Good Golly Miss Molly he'll spin your car 'round!
Without a smile he'll wink his eye.
Killing you softly with flashing light bulbs,
Lifting your soul with a tattoed sigh.

Lyrics by David Essex, 1975

The Merry-go-round (detail) by Ernest Proctor, 1924

T HIS is a little Play, in Three Acts.

Scene: a Toadstool.

Characters: a sentimental Elf
and a wayward Fairy

———

Enter,
an Elf in search of a Fairy.

He finds her,
and this is the consequence.

She runs away,
and this is his condition.

Richard Doyle, *In Fairyland*, 1875

STILL she waited, in her swoon and her drifting, waited, like the Sleeping Beauty in the story. She waited, and again his face was bent to hers, his lips came warm to her face, their footsteps lingered and ceased, they stood still under the trees, whilst his lips waited on her face, waited like a butterfly that does not move on a flower. She pressed her breast a little nearer to him, he moved, put both his arms round her, and drew her close.

And then, in the darkness, he bent to her mouth, softly, and touched her mouth with his mouth. She was afraid, she lay still in his arm, feeling his lips on her lips. She kept still, helpless. Then his mouth drew near, pressing open her mouth, a hot, drenching surge rose within her, she opened her lips to him, in pained, poignant eddies she drew him nearer, she let him come further, his lips came and surging, surging, soft, oh soft, yet oh, like the powerful surge of water, irresistible, till with a little blind cry, she broke away.

D. H. Lawrence, 1885-1930, *The Rainbow*, Ch. XI, 1915

THE KISS (DETAIL) *by Gustav Klimt*, 1907-8

THE KISS

```
        yes         yes
        yes         yes
        yes         yes
        yes         yes
               yes
        yes         yes
        yes         yes
        yes         yes
        yes         yes
```

Ernst Jandl, early 20th century

THE KISS *by Constantin Brancusi*, 1912

SATAN WATCHING THE CARESSES OF ADAM AND EVE *by William Blake*, 1808

THE KISS

THE first kiss was with stumbling fingertips.
Their bodies grazed each other as if by chance
And touched and untouched in a kind of dance.
Second, they found out touching with their lips.

Some obscure angel, pausing on his course,
Shed such a brightness on the face of Eve
That Adam in grief was ready to believe
He had lost her love. The third kiss was by force.

Their lips formed foreign, unimagined oaths
When speaking of the Tree of Guilt. So wide
Their mouths, they drank each other from inside.
A gland of honey burst within their throats.

But something rustling hideously overhead,
They jumped up from the fourth caress and hid.

Karl Shapiro, b.1913

MARISA AND PAUL *by Ken Miller,* 1985

PUNKS KISSING *by John Minihan,* 1980

QUEEN OF KISSES

Come buy my Loves,
   Come buy my Loves,
Monsieur will taste what bliss is!
   I've some will keep,
   Some bright and cheap,
For the coin of this realm is kisses!

Rosemarie Jarski 1993,
inspired by a poem by Thomas Moore, 1779-1852

REINE DE JOIE PAR VICTOR JOZE (DETAIL) *by Henri de Toulouse-Lautrec, 1892*

KISSIN' IN THE BACK ROW OF THE MOVIES

KISSIN' in the back row of the movies
On a Saturday night with you,
Holding hands together, you and I,
Holding hands together, oh yea,
Smoochin' in the back row of the movies
On a Saturday night with you
We could stay forever, you and I,
We could stay forever, you and I,
Hugging and a-kissing in the back row
Of the movies.

Tony Macaulay and Roger Greenaway, 1974

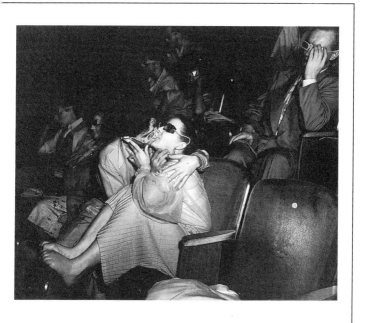

LOVERS *by Weegee*, 1945

LE BAISER *by Umberto Brunelleschi, 1927*

A BOY and girl– they meet – they glance – they kiss.
That's it. Now we can write the scene for this.
I meet you! I behold you! I adore!'
[*He kisses her hand*]
'Oh, let me catch my breath!
I've never been kissed before!
I burn! I faint! I fall!'
'That's Shelley – but not bad at all.
Now passion –'
'Oh, darling! My lips burn until
I've kissed you –'
'You beautiful witch – I can't resist
you.'
'I scream for joy!
Come kiss my lips
And end my inhibitions.'
'Stop! This is too realistic.'

Lorenz Hart, 1895-1943,
from the musical
Music and the Emotions

63

THE KISS IN THE MIRROR *by Elliott Erwitt*, 1955

(YOU'RE SO SQUARE) BABY,
I DON'T CARE

You don't like going to parties
To toot and talk all night long
You just want to park
Where it's nice and dark
And kiss me, sweet and strong
You're so square
Baby I don't care

Jerry Leiber & Mike Stoller

KISS TONGUE-TWISTERS

I saw Esau kissing Kate,
I saw Esau, he saw me.
And she saw I saw Esau.

Tho' a kiss be amiss
She who misses the kisses,
As Miss without kiss,
May miss being Mrs.

Bisquick – Kiss quick!

Kiss her quickly!
Kiss her quicker!

THE ETERNALS *by Julia Lockheart*, 1989

THE sound of a kiss is not so loud as that of a cannon, but its echo lasts a great deal longer.

Dr Oliver Wendell Holmes, 1809-94
from *The Professor at the Breakfast Table*, Ch. 11

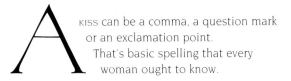

A KISS can be a comma, a question mark
or an exclamation point.
That's basic spelling that every
woman ought to know.

Mistinguett, French dancer 1873-1956

FERRY CROSSING *by Louis Stettner, c. 1959*

T RAVEL, trouble, music, art,
A kiss, a frock, a rhyme –
I never said they feed my heart,
But still they pass my time.
Dorothy Parker, 1893-1967

Iᴛs beak caught firmly in the clam shell,
the snipe cannot fly away of an autumn evening.

A poem on the fan in the picture *tr. Nicholas Bornoff, b.1949*

LOVERS, FROM THE POEM OF THE PILLOW (DETAIL) *by Kitagawa Utamaro, 1788*

Groucho	Where is your husband?
Dumont	Why, he's dead.
Groucho	I'll bet he's just using that as an excuse.
Dumont	I was with him to the very end.
Groucho	No wonder he passed away.
Dumont	I held him in my arms and kissed him.
Groucho	Oh, I see. Then it was murder.

'Duck Soup' (Paramount, 1933)

I wasn't kissing her, I was whispering in her mouth.

Chico Marx's reply to his wife who caught him
kissing a chorus girl

'MIRROR, MIRROR . . .' *Harpo Marx in The Cocoanuts, 1929*

CONVICTION (IV)

I LIKE to get off with people,
 I like to lie in their arms,
I like to be held and tightly kissed,
Safe from all alarms.

I like to laugh and be happy
With a beautiful, beautiful kiss,
I tell you, in all the world,
There is no bliss like this.

Stevie Smith, 1902-71

LOVERS *by Dora Holzhandler,* 1975

3 Seconds d'Éternité (detail) *by Robert Doisneau, 1950*

THE GARDEN

THOUSANDS and thousands of years
Would never suffice
To entice
That small second of eternity
When you kissed me
When I kissed you
One morning in the light of winter
In Parc Montsouris in Paris
In Paris
On Earth
Earth that is a star.

Jacques Prévert, 1900-77 *tr. Rosemarie Jarski*

GIVE me another naughty naughty kiss before we part.

Plautus, c. 254-184 BC
Asinaria, Act v, sc. 2

THE KISS (DETAIL) *by* G. Baldry

Kiss, Kiss, Kiss

Kiss, kiss, kiss, kiss me, love.
Just one kiss kiss will do.
Kiss, kiss, kiss, kiss me, love.
Just one kiss kiss will do.
Why death, why life?
Warm hearts, cold hearts.
Kiss, kiss, kiss, kiss me, love.

Lyrics by Yoko Ono, 1980

JOHN LENNON AND YOKO ONO *by Annie Leibovitz*, 1983

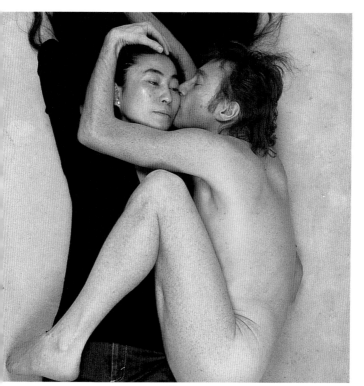

H E kissed her and promised. Such beautiful lips! Man's usual fate – he was lost upon the coral reefs.

Douglas Jerrold, 1803-57

THE SYREN AND THE FISHERMAN (DETAIL) *by Lord Frederick Leighton,*
1857

PAOLO AND FRANCESCA

ONE day we reading were for our delight
    Of Launcelot, how Love did him enthral.
Alone we were and without any fear.
Full many a time our eyes together drew
    That reading, and drove the colour from our faces;
    But one point only was it that o'ercame us.
When as we read of the much-longed-for smile
    Being by such a noble lover kissed,
    This one, who ne'er from me shall be divided,
Kissed me upon the mouth all palpitating.
    Galeotto was the book and he who wrote it.
    That day no farther did we read therein.

Dante Alighieri, 1265-1321
The Inferno, The Divine Comedy tr. Henry Wadsworth Longfellow, 1886

FRANCESCO DE RIMINI (DETAIL) *by William Dyce, c. 1837*

The kiss originated when the first male reptile licked the first female reptile, implying in a subtle, complimentary way that she was as succulent as the small reptile he had for dinner the night before.

F. Scott Fitzgerald, 1896-1940 'The Note-Books', *The Crack-Up*

Above LIZARDS *by Cristóbal Martín Hernández*

KISSING COUSINS

CHARLTON HESTON AND KIM HUNTER *in Beneath the Planet of The Apes,* 1969

PYGMALION

AND he went home, home to his heart's delight,
And kissed her as she lay, and she seemed
warm;
Again he kissed her and with marvelling touch
Caressed her breast; beneath his touch the flesh
Grew soft, its ivory hardness vanishing,
And yielded to his hands, as in the sun
Wax of Hymettus softens and is shaped
By practised fingers into many forms,
And usefulness acquires by being used.
His heart was torn with wonder and misgiving,
Delight and terror that it was not true!
Again and yet again he tried his hopes—
She was alive! The pulse beat in her veins!
And then indeed in words that overflowed
He poured his thanks to Venus, and at last
His lips pressed real lips, and she, his girl,
Felt every kiss, and blushed, and shyly raised
Her eyes to his and saw the world and him.

Ovid,
c. 43 BC-17 AD
Metamorphoses
tr. A. D. Melville,
1986

In the Middle of a Kiss

I n the middle of a kiss
Suddenly it dawned on me
In the middle of a kiss
I knew you were mine.
In the middle of a sweet embrace
That you at first resented
Remember how surprised we were
To find we really meant it.

Song by Coslow & Victoria, 1935

The Embrace *by Bill Arnold*, 1976

PICTURE CREDITS

TEXT ACKNOWLEDGEMENTS

The author and publishers are grateful to the following for permission to reproduce quotations: Bella Godiva Music Inc., copyright 1967, and Music Sales Ltd, for 'Purple Haze' by Jimi Hendrix; BMG Music Publishing for 'Kiss, Kiss, Kiss' by Yoko Ono, © 1980 Lenono Music; Chatto & Windus, a division of Random House (UK) Ltd, for *Henry and Cato* by Iris Murdoch (1976); Éditions Gallimard for 'Le Jardin' from *Paroles* by Jacques Prévert, © Éditions Gallimard 1972; Grafton Books, an imprint of HarperCollins Publishers Ltd, for 'A Poem on The Fan' translated by Nicholas Bornoff from *Pink Samurai* (1991); Harvester Wheatsheaf for 'Hymn to Beauty' by Baudelaire from *Les Fleurs du Mal*, translated by Richard Howard (1982); Leiber & Stoller for '(You're So Square), Baby I Don't Care' by Jerry Leiber and Mike Stoller; Hal Leonard Publishing Corp. and Music Sales Ltd, for 'All My Loving', words and music by John Lennon and Paul McCartney. © Northern Songs 1963, all rights reserved, international copyright secured; Lynkiln Ltd for 'All the Fun of the Fair' by David Essex; New Directions Publishing Corp. and Penguin 20th Century Classics and James MacGibbon, for 'Conviction IV' by Stevie Smith, from *Stevie Smith: Collected Poems* © 1972 by Stevie Smith and *The Collected Poems of Stevie Smith* (1975) respectively; Oxford University Press for 'Pygmalion' by Ovid from *Metamorphoses*, translated by A.D. Melville (1986); Polygram Music Publishing for 'Kissin' in the Back Row of the Movies' by Tony Macaulay and Roger Greenaway; Random House, Inc., New York, for 'The Kiss' from *Poems 1940-1953* by Karl Shapiro; Spring Publications for an excerpt from *The Complete Poems of Catullus*, translated by Jacob Rabinowitz; Viking Penguin, a division of Penguin Books USA, and Gerald Duckworth & Co., for 'Faute de Mieux' by Dorothy Parker from *The Portable Dorothy Parker*, introduction by Brendan Gill, © 1928, renewed © 1956, by Dorothy Parker, and *The Collected Dorothy Parker* respectively.

Every effort has been made to contact the copyright holders of the material quoted; but if any has been inadvertently overlooked the necessary correction will be made in any future edition of this book.